BELLY SONG and Other Poems

BELLY SONG
and Other Poems

by

Etheridge Knight

bp

BROADSIDE PRESS

12651 Old Mill Place   Detroit, Michigan 48238

First Edition
First Printing, July 1973

Copyright © by Etheridge Knight 1973

All Rights Reserved

Library of Congress Catalog Card Number: 72-90098
ISBN: 0-910296-87-1 hardcover $4.95
ISBN: 0-910296-88-X paperback $1.75

Some of these poems have been previously published in **Black World,
Broadside Series, Journal of Black Poetry, New American and Can-
adian Poetry,** and **New Letters.**

Cover photograph, courtesy Judy Ray

Manufactured in the United States of America

Dedicated

"To the People of the Sun"

(two of whom are: my mother,
Belzora Knight Taylor, and my woman,
Mary Ellen McAnally)

(From Wall of Bridgeport, Conn.,
Correctional Center
Dec. 20, 1970)

My friends said, "I'm a junkie."
I said, "You're full of shit!"
  He's dead, he's gone
  He's buried now—
I guess his statement was legit.

                    —Anonymous

Contents

BELLY SONG and Other Poems

ETHERIDGE KNIGHT #32653
Box 41
Michigan City, Ind. 46360
Thurs. nite—Nov. 7, 1968

Lady—

Yeah, well, I made it. Parole. No hip-hip-hoorays, but I do feel good about it—not *grateful,* but good. At least I'll soon be with my woman and children in the larger outside prison. Each day we move closer, Lady.

In one way today's been a bitch; in another way it's been the same-o-same-o. When I got up this morning it was raining, and it's continued all day. I woke up with a headache. After getting myself together, more or less, I stumbled out to breakfast at 6:15. It was still dark. In the mess-hall, I had to say "Yeah" about fifty times to dudes asking me if I thought I'd go/up for parole today. After breakfast I came back to the cellhouse and showered. And then I waited. I had been listed as the ninth man to appear before the parole board, so I expected to be called around 8:30. But it was 10:00 before I was summoned to the "Guard's Hall."

The "Guard's Hall" is a large, barred building that connects the prison proper to the administration building. They form a large "T," with the administration building at the top. The "Guard's Hall" is a busy place—something like a bus station: guys coming and going in to see their counselors, guys going home, and some guys just hanging out. I sat, along with the other men going/up for parole, on a bench near the bottom of the "T." In order to get to the Parole Board Room from the bottom of the "T"—one has to go thru

13

four locked doors to reach the top, then he turns right and goes down a long corridor and knocks (lightly) on a big, brown door.

The first man to be called in was an old brother—must have been in his seventies. He's been here 26 years. Has a full head of snow-white hair—looks kinda/like an old chief. When he turned and disappeared at the top of the "T"— everybody's nerves really came down. One man clipped his fingernails, one got up from the bench and began to pace the floor, another was clicking the top of his cigarette lighter, up and down. But nobody spoke. Then the second man was called to sit in the "Hot Seat"—(a chair situated where the lines of the "T" meet). The old man came out of the corridor. He was smiling. He had made it. The second man got/up and disappeared around the corner. And everybody started talking all at once and lighting/up cigarettes. A few men had to go to the bathroom. And me?—I had to go twice. Finally I was called to the "Hot Seat." From the "Hot Seat" on my right I could see the outside world thru the glass of two locked doors. I saw a car drive up and some people, probably visitors, get out. At last, the guy before me, a gray, came out of the corridor. He had made it. The buzzer sounded. I got up and went down the corridor, past the counselors' offices, and knocked on the door.

The parole board is made up of five men: three ofays, one super/black anglo saxon, and another black who at least wears a mustache, and who is Chairman of the Board. (Oowee, baby, you talking bout tight game!—place a Black as puppet/head and then who can claim that brothers ain't getting a fair shake?)—At any rate, I walk into the room and five dudes are sitting. Solemnly. Bearers of Heavy Burdens. The Chairman asks me if I'm me. I tell him, yes, I'm me. He tells me to sit down. They shuffle some papers and

14

study me; I tremble inside and study them—especially the super/black anglo saxon. Then the Chairman takes me thru the paces, and I respond with the proper "yessirs" in the proper tone, like a well trained thoroughbred. It is clear from the first couple of questions that I'm gonna be given a parole, but the ritual has to be played out. The pins have to be stuck in, until I bleed. I bleed. But it doesn't last long. I smile what I hope is a grateful smile, thank the men, get up and leave. Back in the "Guard's Hall" I see a few of my buddies who have slid in to find out what happened. I give them the sign. I get my Pass from the guard at the gate and go straight to the Deputy's Office to send telegrams to you and mom.

So I made it, and I'm glad. A few more weeks and you'll be stepping/off that plane, scared as hell. . and I'll be standing there waiting for you, scared as hell.

I'm writing to Dudley, Giammanco, Gwen, and Breitman, telling them about my making parole.—And dig: I ran across a book, edited by Breitman: *Trotsky on Black Nationalism and Self Determination,* which cleared up some of the confusion in my mind that Brother Anderson had created with his piece in the latest *Negro Digest.* Hell, I *knew* there was no contradiction between the Black Nation Concept and Revolutionary Nationalism. Trotsky spells it out clearly—clear enough at least to satisfy me at this point. As I said before, perhaps it was just the brother's definition that fucked me up. Did I tell you that Dudley said a Donald Hall wanted to use some of my poems in an anthology? According to Dudley, Donald Hall wrote to LeRoi for some poems too. And LeRoi said, No. The dude couldn't understand that. But I can, I think. That lil cat is the Boss Black Poet and if he's going to contribute his name and poems to white anthologies, he might as well marry a white girl and move to Sweden. Or wherever. His refusal has to be seen as both personal and

15

symbolic—in his case both are probably the same. Black Poets publish thru Black Publishers for Black people. Simple as that. On the other hand—at this point—I see very little wrong with lesser (in terms of reputation) poets allowing their poems to appear in ofay/mixed anthologies. Because you can bet, wherever whitey is (including anthology readers) there'll be some brainwashed brothers, and perhaps the Black poems will pierce their red, white, and blue brains.

Yeah, well . . .

I should be splitting from here around the end of the month. And then it'll be your/time. Your/time. What are you and the children doing tonight? Sometimes I think of you. And the changes. And I want to scream, explode. Yeah. This is gonna be a long drag of a week/end. Monday's a holiday—and I won't hear no sweet words from my woman. Soon, Lady, soon. Gonna go now. Take care of yourself and the children. And always know that I love you.

Always—
Etheridge

Genesis

the skin
of my poems
may be green. yes,
and sometimes
wrinkled
or worn

the snake shape
of my song
may cause
the heel
of Adam & Eve
to bleed. . . .

split my skin
with the rock
of love old
as the rock
of Moses
my poems
love you

Another Poem for Me
(after recovering from an O.D.)

      what now
      what now dumb nigger damn near dead
      what now
      now that you won't dance
      behind the pale white doors of death
      what now   is   to be
      to be what you wanna be
      what you spozed to be
      or what white/america wants you to be
      a lame crawling from nickel bag to nickel bag
      be black brother/man be black
      and blooming in the night
      be black like your fat brother
      sweating and straining to hold you
      as you struggle against the straps
      be black   be black like
      your woman   her pained face floating
      above you   her hands sliding
                       under the sheets
      to take yours be black like
      your mama sitting in a quiet corner
      praying to a white/jesus to save her black boy

      what now dumb nigger damn near dead
      where is the correctness
      the proper posture
      the serious love of living
      now that death has fled these quiet corridors

18

Relaxing
in the Charity Ward at Mercy Hospital

All the old/men
                lie dying
squirming in their own shit
in the Hospital named Mercy

All the old/men
                lie dying
                all day dying
                in the morning dying

When the well/fed/pink cheeked priest
at break of day follows a white/starched nun
thru the Charity/Welfare ward at the Hospital
named Mercy. The fat well fed priest
B
l
e
ss all the old/men who
                lie dying
squirming in their own shit

Huey

Wel/come back, brother
from . .
the House of many Slams
to
these mean bricks

a poet
sung to me:
lets us
drink wine in the alley
and dance in the streets

everyday people
have found
a prince

bright-eyed
wonder-child

comes
Revolution.

On the Yard

A slim
young fascist
fresh from the Hole
slid into me
murdered me
with his eyes
and said, "Man,
why ain't you
doing something?"

All night
I sat up
All night
wrote 5,000 words
explaining how
I
was doing something

but the slim cat—
beautiful fascist
didn't buy
it—nor
did I
completely

At Forty-four

At forty-four years of age
My dancing pa was dead.
"Just went to sleep," my mother cried.
"Peaked out," the doctor said.

A Poem for 3rd World Brothers

So keep your bouncing walk, and.
keep your hip and mellow talk. yeah—and
keep your jackknife laughter that shakes the air.
cause white/america would have you move
like cubes. stumbling. without rhythm
or freedom. white/america would design
your dance and your speech by computer—
would have you sit in stiff chairs
and squeeze your knees.
white/america would kill the cat in you.

or they will send their lackeys to kill for them.
and if those negroes fail
white/america will whip out her boss okie doke:
make miss ann lift the hem of her mystic skirt
and flash white thighs in your eyes to blind you
to your own beauty and that of your sisters
who choke back the hurt and hide their love
behind blonde wigs and red wine.
and if you ain't dead
by the time white thighs wrap round your head

white/america will send the thrill of the pill
to kill you.
you diggit?—you diggit?
to down the red devils is to deal in Blk/death
(makes you fuck over your brothers, (cuts you off
from your people, (makes you cop out
and roam single-o thru this graveyard
of white/america. (and your ears will be deaf
to the cries of Blk/children who look to you to
protect them from the white/ghosts.

So keep your bouncing walk. and.
keep your hip and mellow talk. yeah—and
keep your jackknife laughter that shakes the air.
white/america seeks to kill the cat in you
cause white/america knows that fire eyes glow
that Blk/muscles are strong
and that if brothers dance together
freedom won't be long—
you diggit?—you diggit?

Haiku 2

1

Outside, the thunder
Shakes the prison walls; inside
My heart shakes my ears.

2

(For Sonia)
Snow from the mountains
Of my heart instantly melts
In your warm Blackness.

3

Black men with Torches
Follow the bloody tracks of
The albino beast.

4

Gray jets drag white tails
Across blue skies; gray rats drag
Tails across black legs.

Dark Prophesy: I Sing of Shine

And, yeah, brothers,
while white/america sings about the unsink
able molly brown
(who was hustling the titanic
when it went down)
I sing to thee of Shine
the stoker who was hip
enough to flee the fucking ship
and let the white folks drown
with screams on their lips
(jumped his black ass into the dark sea, Shine did,
broke free from the straining steel).
Yeah, I sing of Shine
and how the millionaire banker stood on the deck
and pulled from his pocket a million dollar check
saying Shine Shine save poor me
and I'll give you all the money a black boy needs—
how Shine looked at the money and then at the sea
and said jump in muthafucka and swim like me—
And Shine swam on—Shine swam on—
how the banker's daughter ran naked on the deck
with her pink tits trembling and her pants roun her neck
screaming Shine Shine save poor me
and I'll give you all the cunt a black boy needs—
how Shine said now cunt is good and that's no jive
but you got to swim not fuck to stay alive—
And Shine swam on—Shine swam on—
how Shine swam past a preacher afloat on a board
crying save me nigger Shine in the name of the Lord—
how the preacher grabbed Shine's arm and broke his stroke—
how Shine pulled his shank and cut the preacher's throat—

And Shine swam on—Shine swam on—
And when the news hit shore that the titanic had sunk
Shine was up in Harlem damn near drunk—
and dancing in the streets.
Yeah, damn near drunk and dancing in the streets.

—Etheridge Knight

A Poem
to Be Recited

A poem
to be recited
while waiting in line to sign/up for your unemployment
    check
or
while standing in line to be fed in the prison mess-hall
or
while boarding a troop/ship for Vietnam
or
while walking thru the playground in "the projects":

The Children in Blk america grow up quickly
(and they die young.
The Children in Blk america grow up quickly
(and they die young.

The Children in Blk america have sad eyes.
The Children in Blk america have sad eyes.
The Children of Blk america are ashamed of their fathers.
The children of Blk america are ashamed of their fathers.

A Poem for a Certain Lady
on Her 33rd Birthday

Who are we
to ride the curves of air
or to worry about the waning moon?
The mountains will not tremble
and the sea will not give up her dead.

Time is now, said the African Poet.
Unfelt as our touch
across these seasons
unending as the circle
of our dead fathers and unborn sons—
the rise and fall of our laughter—
the measure of our steps
as we move
to each other.

Years are strips of tinsel
hanging on hunky brains
Our time is the constant blooming
of our love.

No Moon Floods
the Memory of That Night

No moon floods the memory of that night
only the rain I remember the cold rain
against our faces and mixing with your tears
only the rain I remember the cold rain
and your mouth soft and warm
no moon no stars no jagged pain
of lightning only my impotent tongue
and the red rage within my brain
knowing that the chilling rain was our forever
even as I tried to explain:

"A revolutionary is a doomed man
with no certainties but love and history."
"But our children must grow up with certainties
and they will make the revolution."
"By example we must show the way so plain
that our children can go neither right
nor left but straight to freedom."
"No," you said. And you left.

No moon floods the memory of that night
only the rain I remember the cold rain
and praying that like the falling water
returns to the sky you would return to me again.

Upon Your Leaving
(for Sonia)

Night
and in the warm blackness
your woman smell filled the room
and our rivers flowed together. became one
my love's patterns. our sweat/drenched bellies
made flat cracks as we kissed
like sea waves lapping against the shore
rocks rising and rolling and sliding back.

And
your sighs softly calling my name
became love songs child/woman songs
old as a thousand years new as the few
smiles you released like sacred doves. and I
fell asleep, ashamed of my glow, of my halo, and
ignoring them who waited below
to take you away when the sun rose. . . .

Day
and the sunlight playing in the green leaves
above us fell across your face traced the tears
in your eyes and love patterns in the wet grass.
and as they waited inside in triumphant patience
to take you away I begged you to stay.
"but, etheridge," you said, "i don't know what to do."
and the love patterns shifted and shimmered in your eyes.

And
after they had taken you and gone, the day
turned stark white. bleak. barren like
the nordic landscape. I turned and entered
into the empty house and fell on the floor.
laughing. trying to fill the spaces your love had left.
knowing that we would not remain apart long.
our rivers had flowed together.
we are one.
and are strong.

Feeling Fucked/Up

Lord she's gone done left me done packed/up and split
and i with no way to make her
come back and everywhere the world is bare
bright bone white   crystal sand glistens
dope death dead dying and jiving drove
her away made her take her laughter and her smiles
and her softness and her midnight sighs—

Fuck Coltrane and music and clouds drifting in the sky
fuck the sea and trees and the sky and birds
and alligators and all the animals that roam the earth
fuck marx and mao fuck fidel and nkrumah and
democracy and communism fuck smack and pot
and red ripe tomatoes fuck joseph fuck mary fuck
god jesus and all the disciples fuck fanon nixon
and malcolm fuck the revolution fuck freedom fuck
the whole muthafucking thing
all i want now is my woman back
so my soul can sing

Haiku 1

A slender finger of light
pokes a golden finger
in the bare black stage.

For Mary Ellen McAnally

Who is
a perfect poem
and a song
pulse of love
world of wonders
and the warm black earth
falling
thru my fingers

On Watching Politicians
Perform at
Martin Luther King's Funeral

Hypocrites shed tears
like shiny snake skins

words rolling
thru the electric air

the scent of flowers
mingles with Jack Daniels
and Cutty Sark

the last
snake skin slithers
to the floor where
black baptist feet
have danced in ecstacy

they turn
away
to begin
again

manicured fingers shuffling
the same stacked deck
with the ante
raised

Ilu, the Talking Drum

The deadness was threatening us—15 Nigerians and 1
   Mississippi nigger.
It hung heavily, like stones around our necks, pulling us down
to the ground, black arms and legs outflung
on the wide green lawn of the big white house
near the wide brown beach by the wide blue sea.
The deadness was threatening us, the day
was dying with the sun, the stillness—
unlike the sweet silence after love/making or
the pulsating quietness of a summer night—
the stillness was skinny and brittle and wrinkled
by the precise people sitting on the wide white porch
of the big white house. . . .
The darkness was threatening us, menacing . . .
we twisted, turned, shifted positions, picked our noses,
stared at our bare toes, hissed air thru our teeth. . . .
Then Tunji, green robes flowing as he rose,
strapped on *Ilu,* the talking drum,
and began:

kah doom/kah doom-doom/kah doom/kah doom-doom-doom
kah doom/kah doom-doom/kah doom/kah doom-doom-doom
kah doom/kah doom-doom/kah doom/kah doom-doom-doom
kah doom/kah doom-doom/kah doom/kah doom-doom-doom

the heart, the heart beats, the heart, the heart beats slow
the heart beats slowly, the heart beats
the blood flows slowly, the blood flows
the blood, the blood flows, the blood, the blood flows slow
kah doom/kah doom-doom/kah doom/kah doom-doom-doom
and the day opened to the sound

kah doom/kah doom-doom/kah doom/kah doom-doom-doom
and our feet moved to the sound of life
kah doom/kah doom-doom/kah doom/kah doom-doom-doom
and we rode the rhythms as one
from Nigeria to Mississippi
and back
kah doom/kah doom-doom/kah doom/kah doom-doom-doom

People Poem
(For Patrice Lumumba)

>they ripped him off
>yes they did
>
>all of his kingdoms
>all of his castles
>all of his empires
>all of his dreams
>
>they ripped him off
>yes they did
>they ripped him off
>yes they did

After Watching B. B. King on T.V. While Locked in No. 8 Cell, No. 5 Cage of the Bridgeport, Conn., State Jail

And now man
as you stand there
in the white glare
the sound I hear
from your tuxedoed frame
somehow ain't the same
that's filled my belly and ears
for so many many years
yet the pain on your face is the same
despite the gloss and the glitter and the fame
and the new name:
CULTURE
and now man
with the sound
of your songs still ringing round
these bars in sad procession
I think of some lines from a sonia/poem:
"Blues ain't culture—
they sounds of oppression—
of the game the man's been running
all these years."

Belly Song
(for the Daytop Family)

"You have made something
Out of the sea that blew
And rolled you on its salt bitter lips.
It nearly swallowed you.
But I hear
You are tough and harder to swallow than most. . . ."
                                                    —S. Mansfield

1

And I   and I/must admit
that the sea in you
            has sung/to the sea/in me
and I   and I/must admit
that the sea in me
            has fallen/in love
            with the sea in you
because you have made something
out of the sea
            that nearly swallowed you

And this poem
this poem
this poem/I give/to you.
this poem is a song/I sing/to you
from the bottom
      of the sea
            in my belly

this poem
this poem/is a song/about FEELINGS

about the Bone of feeling
about the Stone of feeling
  and the Feather of feeling

2

This poem/is/
a death/chant
and a grave/stone
and a prayer for the dead:
    for young Jackie Robinson.
a moving Blk/warrior who walked
among us
    with a wide/stride—and heavy heels
moving   moving   moving
thru the blood and mud and shit of Vietnam
moving   moving   moving
thru the blood and mud and dope of America
    for Jackie/who was/

a song
and a stone
and a Feather of feeling
    now dead
and/gone/in this month of love

this poem
this poem/is/a silver feather
and the sun-gold/glinting/green hills breathing
river flowing—for Sheryl and David—and
their first/kiss by the river—for Mark and Sue
and a Sunday walk on her grand/father's farm
for Sammy and Marion—love/rhythms
for Michael and Jean—love/rhythms
love/rhythms—love/rhythms—and LIFE.

for Karen J. and James D. and Roland M. and David P.
                        who have not felt
the sun of their eighteenth summer. . . .

3

And this poem
this poem/is/for ME—for me
and the days/that lay/in the back/of my mind
when the sea/rose up/
                to swallow me
and the streets I walked
                were lonely streets
                were stone/cold streets
this poem
this poem/is/
for me/and the nights
                when I
wrapped my feelings
                in a sheet of ice
and stared
        at the stars
                thru iron bars
                        and cried
in the middle of my eyes. . . .

this poem
this poem
this poem/is/for me
                and my woman
                and the yesterdays
when she opened
                to me like a flower

but I fell on her
        like a stone
I fell on her like a stone. . . .

4

And now—in my 40th year
        I have come here
to this House of Feelings
to this Singing Sea
and I   and I/must admit
that the sea in me
        has fallen/in love
with the sea in you
because the sea
that now sings/in you
        is the same sea
that nearly swallowed you—
        and me too.

Seymour, Conn.
June, 1971

Green Grass and Yellow Balloons
(for Alexandria Keller, a poet at four)

the garden we walked in
was dead/ dying
and the fine/ rain fell
you held/ my hand
fine/ rain falling
cold wind blowing
rain thru your hair
dead world dying
re/ born
by your words
warm and soft and brown
like your eyes
etheridge, you said, i've
composed a poem for you

green grass
and yellow balloons
floating in the sky
you sang of. and sadness too.
softly you sang
your words warming me
and the sea rose in me
and your song sent me spinning
and i thought of e e cummings
mud puddles and colored marbles
and what the fuck was i doing
in this new/ england/ state—
then your eyes seemed sadder to me
and your words seemed warmer to me
and the sea rose higher in me
and suddenly

i was 4 and you were 40
and we were one
as the fine/ rain fell
harder
and harder
and harder
until we came to the white/ fence
that separated
us
from the River

so soon. so soon
do yellow balloons
burst
demons stalk/ this land
that smash
people and poets
whether 4 or 40
so soon. so soon
will your words
be eagles
that rise screaming
from the warmth of their nest
to soar
above this freeze
and froze and frigid land
and we
who walk in new ways
will hear you
we will hear you—
and sing too
of green grass. and yellow balloons

10/ 12/ 71

Untitled 1

1

Before you
my days had two lean faces.
I stripped them bare and stacked
them in the south corner of my mind.
Back to back they stood—
like hostile lovers

2

For Third World Guerrillas, urban or otherwise:

Men who move in mountains
are the first to see the sun,
are the last to see it leave.
Here in the valleys we live in shadows,
here light does not linger late—
early night hides the slender self. . . .

This Poem

This poem is for you
This poem is to inform you
This poem is for you to listen to
who you are/where you at/
This poem is to pull your coat to who
your enemy is and where he's at.
This poem is for all the Black Mothers, wet eyed and weary
watching their children die young, cut down by white america
like young roses broken in a hailstorm
This poem is for all the black Brothers dead and
dying in Vietnam, when they should be marching the
streets of Birmingham
This poem is for you, to comfort you
This poem/is/to help you out of bed when the morning is
cold and the day's work is hard. This poem is to soothe you
when your woman is gone and you're all alone,
This poem is to help you to be a man Now, to move to
Freedom Now,—
This poem is for the junkies nodding on 125th St.
This poem is for the whores walking on Beale St.
This poem is for the brothers in foundries at Ford,
Chrysler, and General Motors.
This poem is for the sisters typing, nursing, cooking,
teaching, and standing on assembly lines.
This poem is a love poem to you.

For Black Poets
Who Think of Suicide

Black Poets should live—not leap
From steel bridges (Like the white boys do.
Black Poets should *live*—not lay
Their necks on railroad tracks (like the white boys do.
Black Poets should seek—but not search too much
In sweet dark caves, nor hunt for snipe
Down psychic trails (like the white boys do.

For Black Poets belong to Black People. Are
The Flutes of Black Lovers. Are
The Organs of Black Sorrows. Are
The Trumpets of Black Warriors.
Let All Black Poets die as trumpets,
And be buried in the dust of marching feet.

Untitled 2

Death seeks first
the fire and earth.
Water and air
always die last.
Lions and Tigers
are doomed at birth.
Eels and sparrows
bloom forth
in the U.S.A.

Jazz Drummer

MAX ROACH
has fire and steel in his hands,
rides high, is a Makabele warrior,
tastes death on his lips, beats babies
from worn out wombs,
                  grins with grace,
and cries in the middle of his eyes.

MAX ROACH
thumps the big circle in bare feet,
opens wide the big arms,
and like the sea
           calls us all.

One Day
We Shall All Go Back
(For Jake & Margaret Milliones, and Nicky & Curtis)

One day we shall all go back—
we shall all go back (down home
to the brown hills and red gullies (down home
where the blood of our fathers
has fed the black earth (down home
where the slow/flowing rivers, dark and silent,
sing to the bones of our brothers (down home
wrapped forever in black wetness (down home. . . .

One day we shall all go back (down home
we shall leave the cold northlands
of icy stares, frozen hearts, stiff snot, cold flats,
racking coughs, hard cash, and go back (down home
to be kissed by sweet rain and warm sun on black backs.

We shall all go back (down home
to avenge Medgar, and Martin, and lil Emmett Till,
and all the others who died the good death (down home—
back—back to avenge our fathers and mothers killed and
    raped
in Natchez, Memphis, Montgomery, Mobile, Lake Charles,
New Orleans, Baton Rouge, Macon, Waycross, Charleston,
Jackson, Savannah, Tougoloosa. . . .

One day we shall all go back—
We shall surely all go back (down home
and the southland will tremble to our marching feet (down
    home
where our freedom cries will shake the southern skies (down
    home
and the shame will leave our children's eyes (down home. . . .

A Poem of Attrition

I do not know if the color of the day
Was blue, pink, green, or August red.
I only know it was Summer, a Thursday,
And the trestle above our heads
Sliced the sun into black and gold bars
That fell across our shiny backs
And shimmered like flat snakes on the water,
Worried by the swans, shrieks, jackknives,
And timid gainers—made bolder
As the day grew older.
Then Pooky Dee, naked chieftain, poised,
Feet gripping the black ribs of wood,
Knees bent, butt out, long arms
Looping the air, challenged
The great "two 'n' a half" gainer. . . .
I have forgotten the sound of his capped
Skull as it struck the block. . . .
The plop of a book dropped? the tear
Of a sheer blouse?
I do not know if the color of the day
Was blue, pink, green, or August red.
I only know the blood slithered, and
Our silence rolled like oil
Across the wide green water.

A Poem for Myself

(Or Blues for a Mississippi Black Boy)

I was born in Mississippi;
I walked barefooted thru the mud.
Born black in Mississippi,
Walked barefooted thru the mud.
But, when I reached the age of twelve
I left that place for good.

My daddy he chopped cotton
And he drank his liquor straight.
Said my daddy chopped cotton
And he drank his liquor straight.
When I left that Sunday morning
He was leaning on the barnyard gate.

I left my momma standing
With the sun shining in her eyes.
Left her standing in the yard
With the sun shining in her eyes.
And I headed North
As straight as the Wild Goose Flies,

I been to Detroit & Chicago—
Been to New York city too.
I been to Detroit and Chicago
Been to New York city too.
Said I done strolled all those funky avenues
I'm still the same old black boy with the same old blues.

Going back to Mississippi
This time to stay for good
Going back to Mississippi
This time to stay for good—
Gonna be free in Mississippi
Or dead in the Mississippi mud.

Prison Graveyard

The dying sun
slides over the tiger teeth
lying row on row
beneath the high and western wall.

And tonight as the keepers
march in the moonlight
the spirits will rise and fret

And fight because no hymns
were sung to soothe
their journey to eternity,
no mourners stood in solemn stance
and wept;

So the spirits dance
the devil's step, and are kept
from riding the winds to the sea.

My Life,
The Quality of Which

My life, the quality of which
From the moment
My Father grunted and comed
Until now
As the sounds of my words
Bruise your ears
IS
And can be felt
In the one word: DESPERATION

But you have to feel for it

June 6, 1972

A Watts Mother Mourns
While Boiling Beans

The blooming flower of my life is roaming
in the night, and I think surely
that never since he was born
have I been free from fright.
My boy is bold, and his blood
grows quickly hot/ even now
he could be crawling in the street
bleeding out his life, likely as not.
Come home, my bold and restless son.—Stop
my heart's yearning! But I must quit
this thinking—my husband is coming
and the beans are burning.

For Eric Dolphy

on flute
spinning   spinning   spinning
love
thru/out
the universe

i
know
exactly
whut chew mean
man

you like
titi
my sister
who never expressed LOVE
in words (like the white folks always d
she would sit in the corner   o
and cry   i
everytime   n
ah   g
got a whuppin

The Bones
of My Father

There are no dry bones
here in this valley. The skull
of my father grins
at the Mississippi moon
from the bottom
of the Tallahatchie,
the bones of my father
are buried in the mud
of these creeks and brooks that twist
and flow their secrets to the sea.
but the wind sings to me
here the sun speaks to me
of the dry bones of my father.

2

There are no dry bones
in the northern valley, in the Harlem alleys
young/black/men with knees bent
nod on the stoops of the tenements
and dream
of the dry bones of my father.

And young white longhairs who flee
their homes, and bend their minds
and sing their songs of brotherhood
and no more wars are searching for
my father's bones.

3

There are no dry bones
here, my brothers. We hide from the sun.
No more do we take the long straight strides.

Our steps have been shaped by the cages
that kept us. We glide sideways
like crabs across the sand.
We perch on green lilies, we search
beneath white rocks. . . .
THERE ARE NO DRY BONES HERE

The skull of my father
grins at the Mississippi moon
from the bottom
of the Tallahatchie.

                              Conn.—Feb. 21, 1971

Evolutionary Poem No. 1

I ain't got nobody
that i can depend on
                    'cept myself

Etheridge Knight Soa
August, 1972
New York City

This Poem is For

NEW YORK CITY
With its 8 million People
Who stand and watch, silently,
A Sister or Brother (Black or White or Yellow or Red)
Being
Raped or robbed—
A Poem for NEW YORK CITY
And for
The Junkies of 115th and Lenox Avenue, for
Madison Avenue jr. executives, for
old ladies and men, with their dogs,
shitting on curbs;

> i pee
> on thee. (period)
>
> —Etheridge Knight Soa

Cop-out Session

I done shot dope, been to jail, swilled
wine, ripped off sisters, passed bad checks,
changed my name, howled at the moon,
wrote poems, turned
backover flips, flipped over backwards,
(in other words)
I been confused, fucked up, scared, phony
and jive
to a whole/lot of people . . .

Haven't you?
        In one way or another?

Enybody else wanna cop-out?
        —Etheridge Knight Soa

A Love Poem

And Mary/is/on the High/Way
coming to me/thru the rain
And the wind.
And.
We are Singing.

—Etheridge Knight Soa
Jeff/City, Mo.—
Sept. 1, 1972

The Last Poem
(that'll be coming at you, thisaway)

'Pears to me   that

WE
Whatever bag we be coming out of
Have
Been
Bullshitting . . . (cepting the Messenger, of course)

Maybe—just maybe . . .
Poet.

—Etheridge Knight Soa

Notice

The
7 Sons Seven
Suns
)
 7)
of Africa

—Etheridge Knight Soa

If you like this book ...BELLY SONG
you will like some of our other books listed on the inside front
cover or on our flyers. You can order them conveniently by mail-
ing this order form.

I enclose $_____ for the books listed below.
(Add 25 cents for postage and handling.)

Author	Title	Price	No. of Copies	Total

Send me free subscription to Newsletter ☐

Send me free announcements of new books ☐

Postage and Handling _____.25

Grand Total $_____

Name_____

Address_____

City_____State_____Zip_____

Mail check or money order to
BROADSIDE PRESS
Dept. M.O., 12651 Old Mill Place   **Detroit, Michigan 48238**